Introduction to China

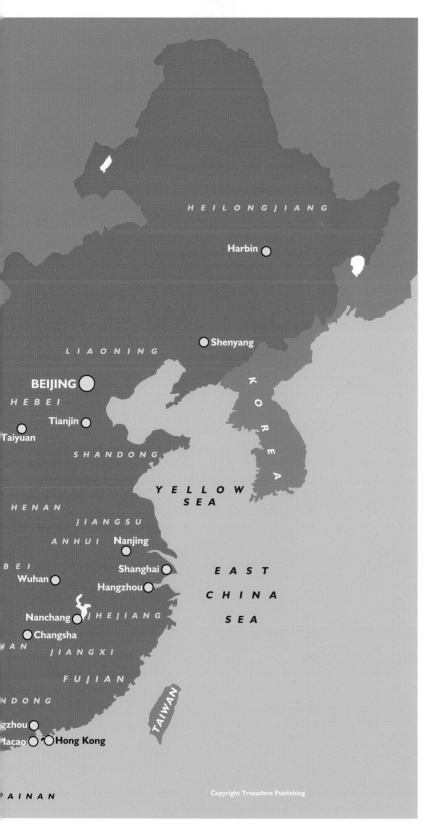

China is a vast and diverse land, rich in culture and with a fabulous heritage. It is the largest of the remaining communist nations, retaining ideology by a combination of pragmatism and authoritarianism. Unlike the European communist states, China has loosened state control sufficiently to allow the entrepreneurial spirit of its people to be satisfied. The country has opened up to outside investment and ideas, although very much on Chinese terms.

In recent years the two European colonial enclaves of Hong Kong and Macau have been returned to China as Special Administrative Regions (SARs). Although China refuses to recognise it, Taiwan remains a separate nation. The Chinese claim it as a renegade province; however, it is highly unlikely Taiwan will ever return to Chinese control.

China ranges from the industrial zones of the south, where rapid growth and entrepreneurial zeal are everywhere, through to the agricultural north, where life remains much as it has always done. In between are the industrial zones of the communist heyday, which are in rapid decline.

Government structure

Mao Zedong, father of the modern Chinese nation. Son of a small landowner, he was born in Hunan province in 1893. In his teens he read the philosophy of Karl Marx. After service with Sun Yat Sen's army, he was a founder member of the Chinese Communist Party in 1921.

Country name	Zhonghua Renmin Gongheguo People's Republic of China (PRC)
Government type	Communist state
Capital	Beijing
Executive branch	
Head of state	President Elected by NPC for five-year term
Head of government	Premier Nominated by president, confirmed by NPC
Legislative branch	Unicameral Quanguo Renmin Daibiao Dahui (National People's Congress) 2979 seats; members elected by municipal, regional and provincial people's congresses to serve five-year terms
Administrative divisions	23 sheng (provinces) 5 zizhiqu (autonomous regions) 4 shih (municipalities) 2 Special Administrative Regions
National holiday	1 October Founding of the People's Republic of China, 1949
Constitution	Original 1949, most recent promulgation 4 December 1982
Legal systems	Mostly a mixture of customary laws and recent statutes
Voting	From 18 years, non-compulsory, universal

Despite all the changes of recent years, China remains firmly under the control of the Communist Party. Its constitution has evolved from the original promulgated in 1949.

There is a unicameral legislature, known as the National People's Congress (NPC), with members, known as deputies, who are elected for a five-year term. The NPC is responsible for overall economic strategy and is able to amend the constitution. However, the NPC never acts without authorisation from the leadership of the Communist Party.

focus on asia

China

VICTORIA MACLEAY

CONTENTS

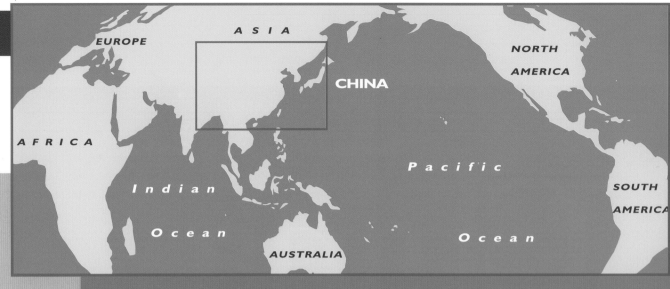

ASIA

EUROPE

CHINA

NORTH AMERICA

AFRICA

Indian

Pacific

SOUTH AMERICA

Ocean

Ocean

AUSTRALIA

China

RUSSIA

KAZAKHSTAN

MONGOLIA

KYRGYZSTAN

XINJIANG

GANSU

QINGHAI

DISPUTED TERRITORY

Xi'a

SHAAN

XIZANG
(TIBET)

● Chengdu

SICHUAN

● Cho

● Lhasa

DISPUTED TERRITORY

GUIZHOU

NEPAL

BHUTAN

● Gu

BANGLADESH INDIA

● Kunming

INDIA

GUANGXI

BURMA

VIETNAM

LAOS

THAILAND

Transport

Public Transport

Although the use of private motor cars is growing rapidly, Chinese people still rely heavily on public transport. Chinese cities boast major bus networks, however the quality varies greatly. Many buses are run down and in need of replacement. Networks of better quality minibuses, with higher fares, have recently been developed.

Urban rail systems are relatively new in China. Only Beijing, Shanghai and Hong Kong offer this form of transport. A system is currently under construction in Guangzhou. Hong Kong's Mass Transit Railway (MTR) is one of the finest urban rail systems in the world. Vast numbers of commuters are moved swiftly and efficiently, with modern and clean trains running at five-minute intervals on most lines.

Taxi services vary greatly in quality throughout China. As a general rule, the larger the taxi, the more expensive the fare. Most are small sedans with meters that might or might not work. Hong Kong taxi services are tightly regulated by the SAR government.

Other types of transport are available in Hong Kong. The private-enterprise trans-harbour Star Ferry provides very frequent and efficient services at a very low price. On Hong Kong island a long-established tramway runs on the northern side from Shaukiewan to Kennedy Town, serving the most heavily populated areas.

Rail

China has a vast, popular rail network covering much of the country. There are 66 000 kilometres of track, about fifteen per cent of which is electrified. Trains are categorised as express, fast or slow. Heavily patronised express trains link all the major cities. During major holiday times such as Chinese New Year, the system is chaotic as people travel to and from their home towns.

Buses and bicycles mingle in a Shanghai street

SCOTT BRODIE

Trams, taxis and double-deck buses provide public transport on Hong Kong island

Guangzhou and Hong Kong are linked by the private-enterprise Kowloon–Canton Railway (KCR), which also operates commuter services in Hong Kong. The KCR is electrified and highly efficient.

CHINA'S RAILWAYS
Total
67 524 km
Standard (1.435 m) gauge
63 924 km
Narrow (0.75 m and 1 m) gauge
3 600 km

Accommodation on long-distance trains is quaintly divided into soft sleeper, soft seat, hard sleeper and hard seat categories. Trains, few of which are air-conditioned, can be very uncomfortable in summer, especially in the south.

It is possible to travel by train from Hong Kong to Moscow. First, passengers go to Beijing to catch the Trans-Manchurian service to Vladivostok or the Trans-Mongolian to Ulaan Baatar. From either of these it is possible to connect to the Trans-Siberian Railway through to Moscow, and then on to other European centres. There are also direct rail links to Hanoi in Vietnam.

Road

Where there is no rail service, long-distance buses link rural areas and towns to the major cities. Like the trains, they are heavily patronised and can be very crowded during peak periods. Bus stations are very chaotic. In summer bus services operate on the Karakoram Highway to Pakistan. Other services link China with Nepal, Tibet and Vietnam.

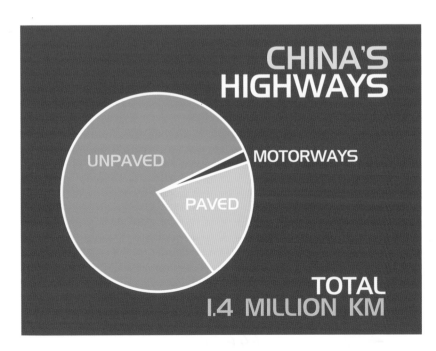

CHINA'S HIGHWAYS
UNPAVED
MOTORWAYS
PAVED
TOTAL
1.4 MILLION KM

The most common form of transport in China is the bicycle. Millions ply the streets of cities and towns all day and night. Although cars are taking over the streets slowly, bicycles still form a large mass of road users. Regulations are generally weighted in favour of bicycle riders.

Car usage is growing in China, especially among the new urban middle class that has arisen since the economic reforms of the 1980s. Most Chinese streets and roads have not been designed for cars, leading to heavy congestion and air pollution. In China cars drive on the right; however, in Hong Kong they drive on the left.

Water

Travel by water is common along the Yangtze, Heilong Jiang and Pearl Rivers. Commuter services of varying quality are provided by large ferries. There are also regular services along the Grand Canal between Beijing and Hangzhou. Large ferries sail regularly from central Hong Kong to Guangzhou. Hong Kong, Macau and Guangzhou are

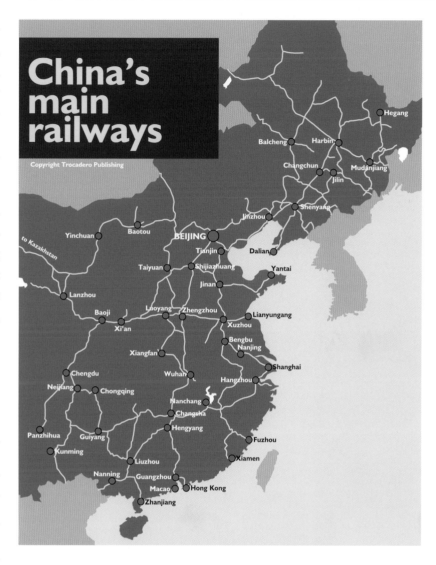

China's main railways

Copyright Trocadero Publishing

A Cathay Pacific aircraft landing at the ultra-modern Hong Kong airport at Chep Lap Kok

CATHAY PACIFIC

also linked by high-speed jet-foil craft carrying passengers in accommodation similar to aircraft.

Aviation

In a country the size of China, air transport is vital. There are three national airlines: Air China, China Southern Airlines and China Eastern Airlines. None is known for its high efficiency or good customer service. Air China (previously called CAAC, for Civil Aviation Administration of China) is the largest. Until the 1980s it was a monopoly, flying domestic services and a wide range of international routes.

China Southern and China Eastern were established in the late 1980s as a result of economic reforms ushered in by Deng Xiao Peng. Initially domestic operators, they have since been granted rights to fly internationally.

Based in Hong Kong is the privately owned Cathay Pacific Airways, one of the world's better airlines. Established in 1946 by an Australian and an American, it has grown into a major operator, linking all parts of Asia and flying to most major centres around the world.

Beijing, Hong Kong, Shanghai, Macau and Guangzhou all have international airports, with airlines from many countries operating to them. Unlike other Chinese airports, Hong Kong's is a highly efficient, vast, modern complex that opened in 1998 on a reclaimed portion of Lantau Island. It is linked to central Hong Kong by a superb high-speed rail service.

CHINA'S SHIPPING FLEET
Barge carrier 2
Bulk 324
Cargo 825
Chemical tanker 21
Combination bulk 11
Combination ore and oil 1
Container 132
Liquefied gas 24
Multifunctional large-load carrier 5
Passenger 7
Passenger/cargo 45
Petroleum tanker 258
Refrigerated cargo 22
Roll-on roll-off 23
Short-sea passenger 41
Specialised tanker 3
Vehicle carrier 1

Communications

hina's telephone system is of varying standards. In the major cities considerable investment has been put into bringing the network up to international standards. However, in rural and regional areas, the quality and service are not what they should be.

Much of the system operates through fibre-optic cables. The use of cellular mobile telephones has grown rapidly in the past decade, but the availability of this service is often restricted outside the major centres. There is also a domestic satellite network using fifty-five ground stations.

Radio and television coverage is good across much of China. Broadcast

access to the potentially lucrative Chinese market.

Access to the internet is closely monitored and service providers are strictly controlled. Even so, the Chinese are enthusiastic users. Around twenty-two million are regular users.

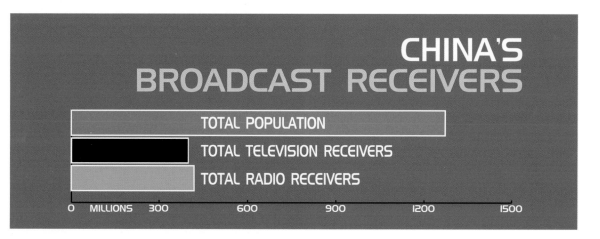

content is rigidly controlled by the government. Nothing that reflects badly on the administration or the Communist Party is put to air.

The availability of international satellite broadcasts is largely restricted to hotels catering to international visitors. Networks such as News Limiteds' Star, based in Hong Kong, have been working for many years to gain

www.sources
www.chinatelecomnews.com
Various articles about telecommunications

www.cctv.com/english
China Central Television site

www.asianinfo.org/asianinfo/
entertainment/tv/china.htm
Many links to television and radio sites

Industry: primary and secondary

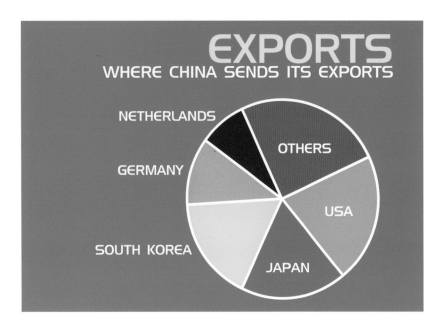

EXPORTS
WHERE CHINA SENDS ITS EXPORTS

NETHERLANDS
GERMANY
SOUTH KOREA
JAPAN
USA
OTHERS

meat. Livestock farming is concentrated in the northern and western regions. Agriculture continues to be very labour intensive, with old-fashioned manual methods and little mechanisation.

Exploitation of mineral wealth forms a substantial part of China's economy. High-quality coking coal is found in abundance in the north and north-east. It is used to generate elec-

More than fifty per cent of China's population is involved in agriculture. Under communism, all agricultural activity was conducted through a collective system in which the community worked as a group to cultivate the land. The economic reforms of the 1980s swept this away, enabling individuals to control their own plots of land. The result was a substantial increase in agricultural yields. Even so, farmers remain one of the poorest groups in Chinese society.

The largest farming areas are in the fertile eastern regions. China is the world's largest producer of rice and wheat, mainly for domestic consumption. It is also a major producer of red

CHINA'S MAIN PRIMARY INDUSTRIES
rice, wheat, potatoes, sorghum, peanuts, tea, millet, barley, cotton, oilseed, pork, fish

CHINA'S MAIN SECONDARY INDUSTRIES
iron and steel, coal, armaments, textiles and apparel, petroleum, cement, chemical fertilisers, footwear, toys, food processing, motor vehicles, consumer electronics, telecommunications

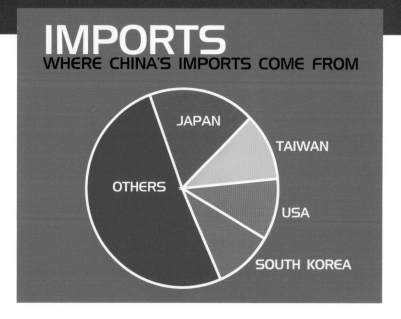

JAPAN

TAIWAN

OTHERS

USA

SOUTH KOREA

tricity and provide power for older industries. Iron ore is found in Liaoning province. Since the 1960s China has become the world's fifth-largest oil producer and a major exporter, with vast deposits off the coast.

In the Communist heyday of the 1950s and 1960s, vast industrial plants produced all kinds of products. Since then Chinese industry has undergone

LONELY PLANET IMAGES — KEREN SU

Shanghai is expected eventually to rival Hong Kong as China's commercial powerhouse

foreign investors could establish factories without the usual Communist controls. The result was rapid development, with efficient factories pouring out all kinds of products that are exported mainly through Hong Kong. The Special Economic Zones have become the wealthiest parts of China.

CHINA'S EXPORTS
US$232 billion
Main exports
machinery and equipment, textiles and clothing, footwear, toys and sporting goods, mineral fuels

a major transformation, mainly through the introduction of international expertise. Today the major growth comes from smaller factories producing consumer goods or high-technology products.

During the 1980s Special Economic Zones were established, mainly in southern China. In these regions

WWW.sources
www.sun-up.com.cn/english/home.htm
Links to wide range of sites on manufacturing
www.mbendi.co.za/indy/ming/as/cj/p0005.htm
Overview of mining in China
www.stats.gov.cn/english
Statistics and data on primary and secondary industries

Geography, environment and climate

The picturesque setting of Guilin

CHINA'S SIZE
Total area
9 326 410 sq. km
Coastline 14 500 km
Border countries
Afghanistan, Bhutan, Burma, India, Kazakhstan, North Korea, Kyrgyzstan, Laos, Mongolia, Nepal, Pakistan, Tajikistan, Vietnam

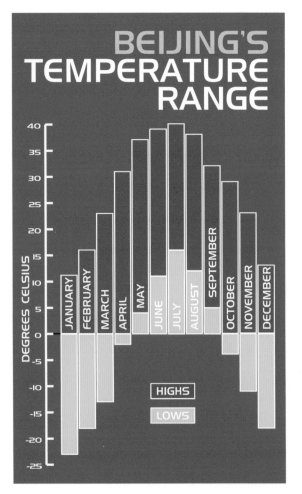

BEIJING'S TEMPERATURE RANGE

HIGHS
LOWS

Geographically, China can be roughly divided into three regions: Xinjiang, the inner-Mongolian tablelands, and the highlands and plains of Manchuria. Eighty per cent of China's population lives in the last, which is broken up into North, Central and South.

Covering such a vast distance from north to south means China's climatic range is huge. Northern winters, influenced by winds from Siberia, are bitterly cold with temperatures dropping to -40°C. Beijing's average daily winter temperature sits at around 0°C. By contrast, a Beijing summer is hot and stifling, with the temperature reaching almost 40°C. In the north, even in summer, nights can be quite cold.

Southern regions tend to be more hot and humid for most of the year. The most uncomfortable period is between May and September. Winter

CHINA'S LOCATION
Latitude 35°N
Longitude 105°E

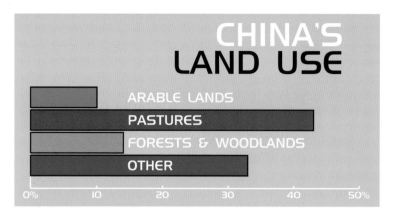

CHINA'S LAND USE

(bar chart)

- ARABLE LANDS
- PASTURES
- FORESTS & WOODLANDS
- OTHER

0%　10　20　30　40　50%

in places such as Guangzhou and Hong Kong can be quite cold, but nothing like that in the north, and it only lasts a few months. Hong Kong during the summer months commonly has temperatures in the high twenties, both minimum and maximum, whether day or night. Central China experiences a short, cold winter and suffers furnace-like heat in summer.

cyclones or hurricanes, they bring powerful winds and lashing rain, sometimes for days. When typhoons approach all activity halts, students and workers are sent home, and everyone waits until the turmoil is over.

The environment is a major problem for China. Rapid development in recent years and poor controls on heavy industry during the core Communist era have delivered a legacy of pollution. Reliance on coal-fired power generation has led to greenhouse gas emissions and acid rain fallout. Untreated wastes have produced some severely polluted waterways. Poor management of land cultivation has resulted in soil erosion. Around twenty per cent of agricultural land has become useless for crops. Factories with poor emission controls and the growth of private car ownership have led to severe air pollution levels.

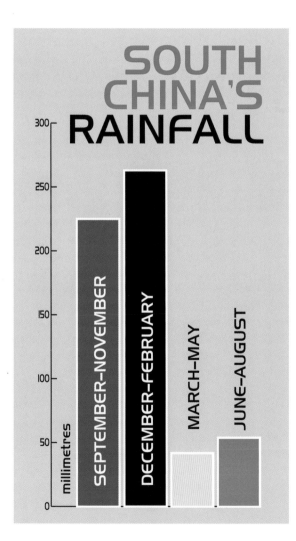

SOUTH CHINA'S RAINFALL

(bar chart, millimetres)

300

250

200

150

100

50

0

- SEPTEMBER–NOVEMBER
- DECEMBER–FEBRUARY
- MARCH–MAY
- JUNE–AUGUST

Southern coastal regions are subject to typhoons, which sweep in from the South China Sea regularly between July and September. Like

www.sources

www.chinaenvironment.net
Discussions and articles on China's environment

www.travelchinaguide.com/climate/
climate and rainfall details

geography.about.com/library/maps/blchina.htm
Wide range of maps and geographical details

Peoples and daily life

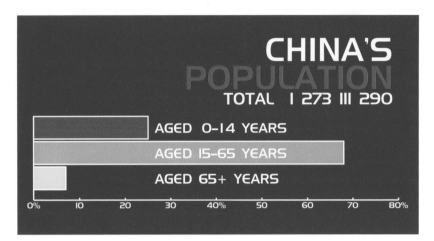

CHINA'S POPULATION

TOTAL 1 273 111 290

- AGED 0–14 YEARS
- AGED 15–65 YEARS
- AGED 65+ YEARS

0% 10 20 30 40% 50 60 70 80%

After the communist take-over in 1949, a program of industrialisation led to considerable dislocation of the population. All through the 1950s people were moved to new industrial areas in Xinjiang, Qinghai, Inner Mongolia and Heilongjiang.

By the 1990s former industrial areas were in decline, being displaced by new and more efficient manufacturing in southern China. A huge

China's ethnic make-up is overwhelmingly Han Chinese. Descendants of the people of the Han Dynasty, they comprise around ninety-two per cent of the population. The rest consists of a wide range of ethnic minorities. These include the Zhuang, Thai-speakers found in Guangxi; the Hui, practising Muslims based around Ningxia; the Uigurs of Xinjiang; and the Yi, whose homeland is on the border of Sichuan and Yunnan.

LONELY PLANET IMAGES — BRADLEY MAYHEW

CHINA'S ETHNIC MIX

- ETHNIC MINORITIES
- KOREANS
- HAN CHINESE

demand for labour caused heavy southern migration, particularly by out-of-work agricultural workers. However, tight government supervision controls entry into these new zones to avoid chaos in housing and infrastructure.

Mandarin is the national and official language of China, although many dialects are spoken, especially in the south. Cantonese is widely spoken in Hong Kong. Other dialects used in the south include Hakka and Wu. Written Chinese is universal, having been adopted in the 1960s as a simplification of the script used for centuries. Hong Kong still uses traditional Chinese script; however, the

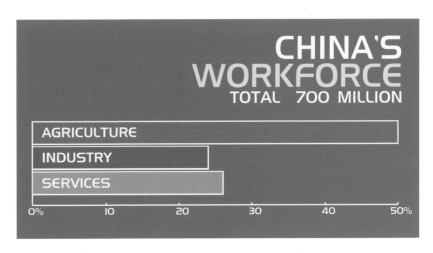

CHINA'S WORKFORCE
TOTAL 700 MILLION

AGRICULTURE	
INDUSTRY	
SERVICES	

0% 10 20 30 40 50%

considerable prosperity, especially in the south. Despite the continuing control of the Communist Party, many areas of China are taking on the appearance of a capitalist society. Shopping malls, expensive restaurants, supermarkets and heavy traffic are all a normal part of life in cities such as Beijing and Shanghai.

Hong Kong is a throbbing capitalist metropolis. However, few ordinary Chinese people will have the chance to see it. The former British colony, along with Macao, are in Special Administrative Zones. Entry is tightly controlled.

People in traditional dress for a festival in Yunnan province

simplified version is now being taught in schools.

Daily life varies enormously across China. For city dwellers it is similar to many other Asian countries; for those on farms it can be a much harder existence. There are pockets of

Religion and beliefs

CHINA'S RELIGIONS

CHRISTIANITY
ISLAM

BUDDHISM & TAOISM

For the Chinese, religion takes the form of a life philosophy to a greater extent than in Western societies. The ancient tenets of Confucianism overlie all aspects of Chinese life. It creates a life framework as much as a religious belief.

Buddhism and Taoism are both strong in China. Lao Tzu founded Taoism, the only indigenous Chinese religion, about 2600 years ago. Legend says he was conceived by a shooting star and carried in his mother's womb for eighty-two years, to be born a wise old man. Seeking solitude and communion with nature in Tibet later in life, he wrote the *Tao Te Ching* (*The Way and its Power*).

Taoism and Confucianism tend to merge. Followers of Tao make liberal use of the Confucian structure in daily life. Tao is said to be the origin of creation and following it enables a person to live life in harmony with nature and the universe.

Confucianism is less spiritual and more practical, providing followers with a social and ethical structure for life. Confucius was born in 551 BC in Shandong province. His teachings were adopted by emperors as the state religion until the collapse of the Qing Dynasty in 1911. Confucius's primary concern was stability through efficient government and systems, espousing respect for self and others.

Under communism, religious practice is discouraged. China's religions have the advantage that they are personal, not requiring vast cathedrals or mosques for services. Instead, individuals worship before a shrine in the home, avoiding an overt challenge to the state.

The principal religious confrontation is provided by Falun Gong, which was banned by the government in 1999. With a basis in Buddhist philosophy, Falun Gong has actively challenged the government's human rights record through demonstrations and public protests. Members have been imprisoned for long periods.

WWW.SOURCES

www.academicinfo.net/chinarelig.html
Large database on religion in China

www.geocities.com/chinesevenice/infotao.htm
History of Taoism

www.europeaninternet.com/china/
underst/christm.php3
Brief details on China's religions

Food and cuisine

Chinese food is known and loved around the world, a testimony to its flavours, diversity and simplicity. Food forms a central part of Chinese life, with the range of cuisines varying from region to region. Chinese people can be very discriminating about quality, as it is believed a good meal promotes mental harmony and physical well-being.

The most common form of cooking is stir-fry. It was developed to save cooking fuel, which was expensive and scarce. The idea was to prepare all ingredients in advance and spend only a short time on the cooking. Meat and vegetables tend to be cooked together.

Beijing is most famous for Beijing (or Peking) Duck, a luxury item because of the time and care it takes to prepare. Cantonese food is steamed, boiled or stir-fried, and uses a minimum of oil. Sichuan province is justifiably famous for its spicy cuisine, which uses chilli and peanuts as core ingredients.

Noodles, popular and easy to prepare, come in three main types: egg, wheat and rice flour. Generally they are combined with other ingredients in a dish, or can be served as part of a soup.

Tea is immensely popular in China, where the flavours of the tea leaf were first discovered. Most meals have tea served as a key component.

www.sources

www.index-china-food.com
Lots of recipes and descriptions of Chinese foods

www.travel.com.hk/china/food.htm
Information about various Chinese cuisines

www.index-china-food.com/tea-culture.htm
All about tea in China

Arts and crafts

A superb example of
Qing Dynasty porcelain

www.sources
www.index-china.com/index-english/arts-g.html
Information on a wide range of Chinese arts and crafts

abe.www.ecn.purdue.edu/~agenhtml/
agenmc/china/china.html
Arts and related matters

www.china-contact.com/www/art.html
Arts, painting, creative pursuits

The talent and workmanship of Chinese artists and craftspeople have been celebrated around the world for centuries.

Highly sought after today are fine examples of the jade carver's work. This beautiful cool green stone has been worked into many elaborate or simple display pieces. Such carvings command high prices from collectors.

Folk arts still thrive in modern China, although they have their roots in ancient history. They include all types of paper crafts such as folding, sculpting and engraving. Paper-related crafts are also used in making kites and coloured lanterns.

Embroidery and related cloth arts flourish in China. All manner of elaborate decorations are created for pillows, bags, cushions and simple decorative pieces. They can be done on silk or other fabrics. Knitting is also popular, with elaborate techniques used to produce magnificent display pieces.

Carvers and sculptors work in a variety of materials, the most popular being jade, wood and bamboo. Some fine designs are developed for puppets, masks and decorative figures. Sculpting is done in clay and pottery for ornaments and children's toys.

China's porcelain makers, particularly those of Jiangxi, Hunan and Hebei provinces, are justifiably famous around the world. Their elegant and delicate works are often fired in kilns built many centuries ago. Such was the quality of Chinese porcelain that 'china' became the generic term for all tablewares.

History and politics

The early dynasties

The earliest evidence of modern Chinese humankind appeared around 20 000 years ago in the northern Ordos region. By 4000 years ago a mostly homogeneous Chinese culture was well established. What variations there were occurred mostly in the south.

The first records of Chinese history are from 3500 years ago when the Shang Dynasty was established. The Shang, centred on the Huanghe and Weihe rivers, lived in a highly class-conscious society. The emperor and his nobles were at the top; the artisans, priests and warriors in the middle; and farmers and slaves at the bottom.

CHINA'S DYNASTIES	
Xia	c. 1994 – c. 1523 BC
Shang or Yin	c. 1523 – c. 1122 BC
Zhou	1122–221 BC
Warring States period	403–221 BC
Qin	221–206 BC
Han	202 BC – AD 220
Three Kingdoms	AD 220– 265
Jin	265– 420
Sui	589– 618
Tang	618– 907
Five Dynasties and Ten Kingdoms	907– 960
Sung	960–1279
Yuan	1271–1368
Ming	1368–1644
Qing or Manchu	1644–1912

At around 1122 BC Shang was conquered by the Zhou Dynasty. Land was divided up among various nobles, creating a feudal regime. Over the next 750 years Zhou produced a number of philosophers, the most prominent being Gong Fuzi (Confucius) and Lao Tzu. During this time the foundations of Chinese culture and ethics developed.

The succeeding Qin Dynasty was at first led by thirteen-year-old Zheng, who grew into a cunning and ruthless emperor. He created a new capital at Xi'an where all nobles were required to live, away from their supporters and armies. Zheng's empire was divided into forty-two provinces,

Emperor Tai Zhu, founder of the Sung Dynasty

THE GREAT WALL

The Qin Dynasty built the Great Wall to keep out the warlike Xiongu from the north. These nomads regularly staged guerrilla raids into Qin territory. One million peasants, convicts and slaves laboured on the wall, which is about 2400 kilometres long.

each with a civil governor. To ensure no uprisings against the emperor, the imperial army was the only military body permitted.

The Han Dynasty

Around 200 BC, after one of numerous rebellions, Zheng was forced to commit suicide. This plunged China into civil war from which two leaders emerged: Xiang Hu, who declared himself emperor of Chu, and Liu Bang, who claimed he was now emperor of Han. After four years of conflict Xiang Hu committed suicide. Liu Bang founded the Han Dynasty, from which all Chinese are considered to have descended.

There followed 400 years of relative peace, during which some fine artistic traditions were established. Chinese explorers penetrated to the Caspian Sea region and northern India. They returned with breeding stock of horses, which greatly enhanced China's military power. A trade route between East and West, known as the Silk Road, developed soon afterwards.

Apart from trade, the new routes to the West brought missionaries.

Indian traders introduced Buddhism, which was adopted enthusiastically by many Chinese. The Han Dynasty was relatively liberal about religion, so Buddhism soon had a major foothold in China, presenting a serious challenge to Confucianism.

Han introduced a system of appointment to important positions based on merit alone. Examinations were developed to test the abilities of those males wishing to enter the civil service. Schools opened across the empire to cater for the new need for knowledge. Success in examinations guaranteed a route to influence and prosperity.

Period of turmoil

When Han collapsed the empire split into three warring factions: Wei, Shu and

Burning books considered critical of the Qin Dynasty

Wu. Eventually Wei emerged superior and the Jin Dynasty was established in AD 265. It lasted until 317, when a period of turmoil began. For more than a century the imperial system persisted shakily in the south, while nomad tribes controlled the north.

In 439 General Wang Qian reunited China under his Sui Dynasty. It lasted until 618 before collapsing under the weight of its corruption and rebellions. Li Yuan, a nobleman, led a force that captured Chang'an. He then founded the Tang Dynasty, in place from 618 to 907.

Tang and Sung

Under Tang the territory of China was expanded to its greatest extent. Central government was reinstated and, for the first time, a standard language brought unity to the vastness of China. Confucianism once more became the guiding philosophy.

Tang's collapse in 907 led to a period known as the Five Dynasties, which lasted fifty years. During this time various military leaders set themselves up in separate empires.

Chaos reigned until 960 when the Sung Dynasty was established, ushering in a new period of progress and artistic development. During Sung, printing processes greatly improved with the introduction of movable type. Also of significance, gunpowder was introduced into warfare.

Kublai Khan

Sung lasted until 1276. For many years China was under almost constant siege by the Mongol

Kublai Khan's forces attack a Chinese city

armies of Genghis Khan. Eventually all of China was under Mongol control, led by Genghis's grandson Kublai Khan, who founded the legendary Yuan Dynasty.

Kublai launched a program of major public works, constructing networks of canals and roads. Despite trying hard to win over his Chinese subjects, he had to rely on Mongol and Turkish administrators to keep the empire under control. He made Beijing the capital and converted to Buddhism. Trade and commerce were encouraged, with a system of currency. Also during this time Marco Polo arrived from Europe.

Ming Dynasty

After Kublai's death in 1294, Yuan declined rapidly. A former Buddhist monk, Zhu Yuanzhang, led an army that drove the Mongols from Beijing in 1368. The Ming Dynasty, which he established, was marked by a return to the qualities of the Sung Dynasty.

Ming lasted until 1644. In the early fifteenth century the 600-hectare Imperial City was completed at Beijing. Within this was the Forbidden City, into which only the emperor, his family and staff could enter.

European intruders

During Ming a very reluctant China was confronted in the sixteenth century by Portuguese

The European trading compound at Guangzhou in 1830

mariners demanding trading rights. After numerous clashes of cultures, Portugal was granted an enclave in southern China, at Macau. Here they established warehouses and homes and discovered good profits could be made by importing opium from India.

The Portuguese were followed by the Spanish, then the Dutch in

1604. The Dutch were more pragmatic than the Portuguese. Having agreed to pay tribute to the Ming emperor, they were granted trading rights. As well as dealing with the Chinese, the Portuguese and Dutch regularly fought each other.

The Qing Dynasty

The demise of Ming was brought about by the steady southward encroachment of the Manchu people, who created the Qing Dynasty. Like the Mongols, the Manchus ruled China by military force. Qing was the last of the Chinese dynasties, although its collapse would be almost three hundred years in coming.

The Opium Wars

In 1757 Emperor Qian Long blocked the access of European traders to all Chinese ports other than Guangzhou. Barter trading was terminated; all goods had to be paid for in silver. However, when the British East India Company discovered Chinese merchants would accept opium in place of silver, trade resumed. Opium grew abundantly in British-controlled Bengal.

By 1839 there were more than two million opium addicts in China. The emperor appointed Lin Zexu to end the opium trade. The Chinese seized the stocks of opium from the traders in Guangzhou, provoking what became known as the Opium Wars. In mid-1840 a British naval force arrived off Guangzhou, escorting ships loaded with opium to pay for the season's crop of tea. In huge demand in England, tea was grown only in China.

After a number of sea battles British troops landed and made their way inland. By June 1842 Shanghai had been captured and Nanjing was set to fall. On 29 August the defeated Chinese signed the Treaty of Nanjing. Among the provisions, Hong Kong was ceded to Britain, and Guangzhou, Fuzhou, Xiamen, Ningbo and Shanghai were opened to trade.

The Second Opium War occurred in 1856–57. A minor incident on the Pearl River sparked an assault on the imperial government by British forces. This led to the Treaties of Tianjin, which opened up more ports to foreign trade and allowed Christian missionaries to travel and preach anywhere in China.

The Taiping Rebellion

The Qing Dynasty was already weakened by decades of internal unrest. The disastrous Opium Wars made things worse. One outcome was the Taiping Rebellion of 1851, led by Hong Xiu Quan, who planned to convert China to Christianity.

By September 1851 his armies had captured Yongan. The following year they swept through much of Hunan province, eventually making Tianjing their main base. Trying to force further concessions from the emperor, the Europeans gained much from the chaos created by Hong. When they had what they wanted, the foreigners joined with Chinese forces to destroy the Taiping rebels.

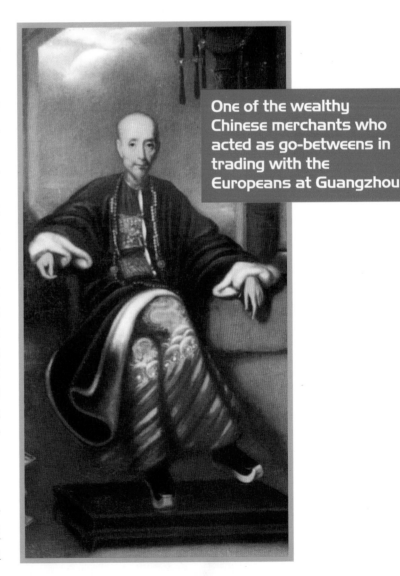

One of the wealthy Chinese merchants who acted as go-betweens in trading with the Europeans at Guangzhou

THE BOXERS
Yihequan
The Society of the
Righteous and Harmonious Fists

Japanese invasion

The Japanese invaded Korea in 1894, driving the Chinese out and securing the Treaty of Shimonoseki. This gave access for Japanese traders to Chinese ports. It also handed over Formosa (Taiwan), the Pescadore Islands and the Liaodong Peninsula to Japan.

Rise of the dowager

Following the Opium Wars and the Taiping Rebellion, China came under the control of the dowager empress Ci Xi. At first she exercised power through her son, Tong Zhi. He was under age when he inherited the throne, and died of smallpox at eighteen. Ci Xi replaced him with her three-year-old nephew, Guang Xu.

Although closely controlled by his aunt, Guang Xu as a young man came under the influence of those who wished to modernise China. In 1898 he established a university and many schools, scrapping the old civil service examinations. Manufacturing was encouraged, a banking system introduced, and free speech permitted.

The Boxers

Ci Xi wanted none of this reform; all she wished for was that the foreigners be expelled. She had the emperor arrested and took control herself once again. In 1900 Ci Xi orchestrated the Boxer Rebellion, staged by members of the Yihequan secret society dedicated to throwing the foreigners out of China.

They massacred Christian missionaries and their converts before laying siege to the European legations in Beijing. The Japanese and German ambassadors were assassinated. The foreigners withstood the siege for fifty-five days before reinforcements arrived and repelled the Boxers.

Demise of the dowager

Ci Xi and Guang Xu fled Beijing in fear of their lives. She returned in 1902, proposing a major program of modernisation, but it was not enough to halt the terminal decline of the imperial system. The reform

Ci Xi, the dowager empress, in 1903

movement, led by Dr Sun Yat Sen, was aided by the death of Guang Xu in 1908. Ci Xi, having replaced him with two-year-old Pu Yi, died a day later, leaving the system in chaos.

End of empire

Following a bomb blast at Wuhan in 1911, revolution spread across the nation. The child emperor and his court were forced out of Beijing. On 29 December Sun Yat Sen was made provisional president of a Chinese republic. China's imperial system had ended and the Qing Dynasty had fallen.

Sun Yat Sen resigned a year later in favour of Yuan Shih Kai, believing only this military leader could unite all China. Yuan's government was marked by authoritarianism and brutality, provoking a number of unsuccessful revolts.

A new emperor

When the Kuomintang (KMT) — National People's Party — was formed in 1912, Sun Yat Sen pledged his support. The following year it won a majority of seats in the National Assembly. Yuan Shih Kai, fearing Sun's influence, expelled KMT members from the assembly and declared himself dictator. Yuan saw himself as the new emperor of China.

Japan, seeing an opportunity to expand its dominion, landed troops in Germany's Shandong territory in 1914. Yuan was forced to accept a list of demands intended to make China subservient to Japan. Following the Great War (1914–18) in Europe Japan

Yuan Shih Kai

was awarded Shandong province by the Versailles Conference.

In December 1915 Yuan declared himself emperor of the Hong Xian Dynasty. It lasted less than three months, as provincial governors rebelled against his rule. When Yuan died in 1916 China became unstable. Warlords who controlled various parts of the country now saw an opportunity to increase their power and their wealth.

The Communists

In July 1921 twelve men met secretly in Shanghai to form the Communist Party of China, with Chen Duxiu as its secretary. Supported by the Soviet Union (USSR), they planned to infiltrate trade unions and worker groups. As there was no aid coming from the Western powers, Moscow persuaded Sun Yat Sen to cooperate with the Chinese Communists.

Civil wars

Following Sun's death from cancer in 1925, KMT leadership passed to Chiang Kai Shek. Determined to break the power of the northern warlords, he assembled a 100 000-strong army. With communist support he led the force north in July 1926. Shanghai fell in March 1927, followed by much of the warlord-dominated territory.

Chiang turned on his Communist allies. Many of the leaders were executed and Communist-allied worker organisations were targeted. After widespread bloodletting the Communists fled to set up a base in Jiangxi province.

Shanghai at the beginning of the twentieth century

The Long March

Chiang threw everything he could muster at the mountainous hideaway. Eventually, in October 1934, the Communists found themselves losing the battle. Mao Zedong and 100 000 supporters embarked on what became known as the Long March.

For a year they contended with unrelenting pressures from the Nationalists and China's climate and geography. Only 7000 arrived in Shaanxi province at the end of the 9500-kilometre march.

Japan invades again

With Chiang battling the Communists, Japan took the opportunity to invade Manchuria in 1931. From this base they moved south. While Chiang preferred to defeat the Communists first, many Nationalists disagreed. In December 1936 they staged the Xi'an Incident. Chiang was kidnapped in an effort to force him into an alliance with the Communists against the Japanese.

The Communists agreed to work with the Nationalists. However, the far better disciplined Communist army was much more effective than Chiang's corruption-ridden forces. The Communists took the opportunity to liberate millions of peasants, winning them over to the cause. Communism's image was also aided by the brutality displayed by the Japanese invaders.

The final clash

When Japan declared war on the Western Allies in 1941, China received considerable military support from the United States. Once World War II ended the shaky Communist–Nationalist truce fell apart.

After Japan's surrender the Soviet Union occupied Manchuria. When the time came for them to depart, they handed the territory to the Communists. From this base they attacked the southern Nationalist-held regions. Shenyang fell to the Communists in November 1948.

It now became obvious Chiang Kai Shek's forces, despite considerable US support, were losing the struggle. Heavy-handed repression of the population, combined with economic instability and famine, tipped the balance in favour of Mao Zedong's Communists.

Communist forces won their greatest psychological victory in January 1949 when Beijing fell with minimal fighting. Other major cities followed during the rest of that year. Mao declared China under Central Communist government on 1 October 1949, under the name of the People's Republic of China.

Off to Formosa

Nationalist forces crumbled as Communist control spread across China. Protected by the US Navy's Seventh Fleet, Chiang and his remaining supporters fled to the island of Formosa (now Taiwan). There, in December 1949, a Nationalist government was established.

While both the Communists and the Nationalists claimed to be the official government of China, the Communists occupied the large bulk of the country. Their government was legitimised by official recognition from Britain, India and other nations. The United States, however, maintained that Chiang's Taiwan-based regime was the legitimate ruler of China.

The Communists moved quickly, consolidating their power and cleaning out the last pockets of Nationalist resistance. Many people fled China, pouring into the British enclave of Hong Kong. While some went on to other parts of the world, many stayed to create the economic powerhouse that Hong Kong became.

Communist China

Mao and the Communists launched a classic communist-style government. Economic intervention brought runaway inflation under control and problems of food distribution were gradually sorted out.

During the 1950s individual ownership of farms was abolished and a collective system introduced. All industry was nationalised and substantial aid flowed in from the Soviet Union. Industrialisation was promoted to ensure independence from the non-communist world.

As part of the Communist conversion, cadres were dispatched to all parts of China. Setting up in villages, they conducted trials of those considered to be exploiters of the peasants: landlords, moneylenders, black marketeers. Some were converted to the cause; as many as two million were executed.

Having been allies during World War II, Mao Zedong (left) and Chiang Kai Shek celebrate victory

The Korean War

China became a major player in the Cold War in October 1950. On the Korean peninsula, United Nations forces had pushed the invading North Korean army out of the south and were pursuing it towards

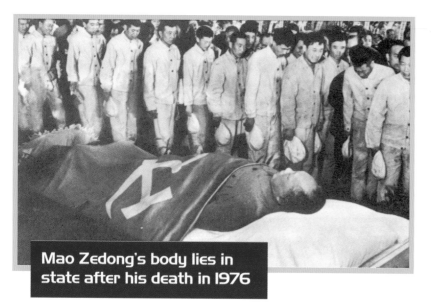

Mao Zedong's body lies in state after his death in 1976

the Chinese border. To defend North Korea the Chinese army swept across the Yalu River, driving General Douglas MacArthur's forces into an ignominious retreat.

The Great Leap Forward

In 1958 Mao launched the Great Leap Forward, aiming to make China a world industrial power. Farming collectives were plundered for labour, separating families and causing much distress. Excessive haste and bad planning led to poor-quality production.

Simultaneously, a much-reduced agricultural labour force could not plant sufficient crops, or harvest them, between 1959 and 1961. Widespread famine resulted. As many as fifty million people may have perished for lack of food during this time.

Breaking with the Soviets

After its hard-line leader Josef Stalin died in 1953, the Soviet Union improved its relations with the non-communist world, particularly western Europe. As China hotly opposed such changes, relations between the two communist giants deteriorated.

With the breach apparently irreparable, by 1960 the Soviet Union had withdrawn all technical assistance to China and ceased aid payments. There was a distinct possibility of war between the two. Soviet and Chinese armies faced each other across their long border in China's north. While minor battles were fought, there was never a major clash.

Spreading the word

China promoted communist movements in other parts of Asia, notably Indonesia, Malaya and Thailand. Initially a supporter of the Vietnamese communists, the relationship soured when Vietnam moved closer to the Soviet Union. Initial support for China among non-communist Asian nations soon evaporated when Chinese-supported groups attempted to overthrow their governments.

Military interventions gradually gave way to diplomatic measures. The Chinese became competitors with the Soviet Union, promoting communism in impoverished nations. Chinese technical advisers were a common sight in poor Asian and African nations in the 1960s and 1970s.

The Cultural Revolution

By the mid-1960s splits were appearing within the Communist Party as various factions jockeyed for power. Mao's status had been damaged by the failure of the Great Leap Forward. To recover he launched the Cultural Revolution in 1966.

Fanatical young Mao supporters, known as Red Guards, were encouraged to bring the nation back to the pure ideals of the 1949 revolution. This was Mao's way of quashing any challenge to his leadership. It did incalculable harm as zealous Red Guards tore the nation apart searching for 'traitors'.

Challenging Mao

In 1971 Defence Minister Lin Biao died in an air crash. It was claimed he was fleeing to the Soviet Union after a failed attempt to assassinate Mao. It is more likely Lin was assassinated because he was close to overthrowing Mao as chairman.

Two Chinas

Under pressure from the United States, the United Nations (UN) maintained Taiwan (the Republic of China) as the official representative of China in the General Assembly. Reality dawned in 1971 when Taiwan was expelled and the People's Republic replaced it.

The United States had proposed a 'two Chinas' policy, with both nations taking seats in the UN. China's growing strength as an economic and political power forced the USA to soften its attitudes. These changes were illustrated dramatically in February 1972, when President Richard Nixon visited Beijing.

Moving for changes

By the 1970s hard-line Chinese communism was disappearing under the more liberal Deng Xiao Peng and Zhou En Lai. On the opposite side the Gang of Four, one of whom was Mao's wife, pushed the pure communist ideology. Mao, still the great figurehead, was torn between the moderates and the Gang.

When Zhou died, the Gang of Four convinced an ageing Mao that Deng's modernisation compromised Mao's revolutionary ideals. Deng was purged from the leadership in 1976, and replaced by Hua Guo Feng. After Mao's death in September the liberals

Deng Xiao Peng (centre) at a party congress

NEWSPIX — STEPHEN SHAVER

A military police officer stands guard at Tiananmen Square

turned on the Gang of Four, who were themselves purged.

Deng returned to power in 1977 as deputy chairman. In reality, he was the most powerful man in China. A major modernisation plan created a favourable atmosphere for foreign companies to invest in China. The collective farms system ended, leading to healthy increases in agricultural production. Special Economic Zones were created in which foreign companies could establish factories.

Colonial hand-over

In 1984 British Prime Minister Margaret Thatcher caved in to Chinese pressure for the return of Hong Kong to China. It was agreed the dynamic city would be returned in 1997 when the 99-year lease on the New Territories expired. Similarly, negotiations with Portugal ended with an agreement for Macau to become part of China once again in 1999.

Tiananmen Square

In 1989 General Secretary Hu Yao Bang died and was replaced by Zhao Zi Yang. Zhao was in turn replaced after a short time by Li Peng. These changes sparked, in April 1989, a series of student-led protests in Beijing's Tiananmen Square.

Having tolerated demands for democratic reform for a time, the government sent in troops who violently broke up the gatherings. Thousands died and many more were arrested, sparking international outrage. Subsequent economic sanctions had a dramatic effect on China's growing economy. China made an effort to win back international support, although relations with many nations remain prickly.

Taiwan

Taiwan's status remains an international problem. The United States continues to support its existence and has pledged military support in the event of an invasion by China. Taiwan is now a major economic power and very wealthy. Less than twenty per cent of its population wants reintegration with China. Even so, China still regards it as a renegade province and regularly conducts military exercises designed to harass the Taiwanese people.

WWW.sources

www.asterius.com/china/
Concise history of China

www.china-contact.com/
www/history.html
Links to various China history sites

Statistics

Total population
1 273 111 290
Birth rate
15.9 per 1000 population
Death rate
6.7 per 1000 population
Infant mortality rate
28.1 per 1000 live births
Life expectancy
male 70 years
female 74 years

GDP growth rate 8%
GDP per capita US$3600
GDP by sector
agriculture 15%
industry 50%
services 35%

Labour force 700 million
Labour force by sector
agriculture 50%
industry 24%
services 26%
Unemployment rate 10% plus

Land area 9 326 410 sq. km
Lowest point
Turpan Pendi — -154 m
Highest point
Mount Everest — 8850 m

Primary industries
rice, wheat, fish, potatoes, sorghum, tea, millet, barley, cotton, oilseed, pork, peanuts
Secondary industries
iron and steel, coal, cement, chemical fertilisers, machine building, armaments, consumer electronics, textiles and apparel, petroleum, footwear, toys, food processing, automobiles

China's flag was adopted following the Communist take-over. The red background represents the Communist spirit. The large star stands for the Communist Party. The four stars are the peasants, workers, bourgeoisie and patriotic capitalists working together to further the revolution.

Natural resources
coal, iron ore, petroleum, natural gas, aluminum, mercury, tin, tungsten, magnetite, antimony, manganese, molybdenum, vanadium, lead, zinc, uranium

Exports US$232 billion
Major exports
machinery, textiles, clothing, footwear, toys, sporting goods, mineral fuels
Imports US$197 billion
Major imports
machinery, mineral fuels, plastics, iron, steel, chemicals

Official languages
Mandarin
Yue, Wu, Minbei, Minnan, Xiang, Gan, Hakka dialects
Currency
Yuan
Religions
Taoism, Buddhism, Islam, Christianity

Index

Focus on Asia: China   ISBN 0 86415 437 2
Published by   Franklin Watts 96 Leonard Street   London EC2A4XD
Created and produced by Trocadero Publishing   Copyright © 2002 S and L Brodie   Printed in Hong Kong